Freddy Sinclair's Double Dare

Written by Bethanie Campbell

Illustrated by Jaclyn Ciurciu

**Foreword by Doc Hendley,
Founder and Author of**
Wine to Water

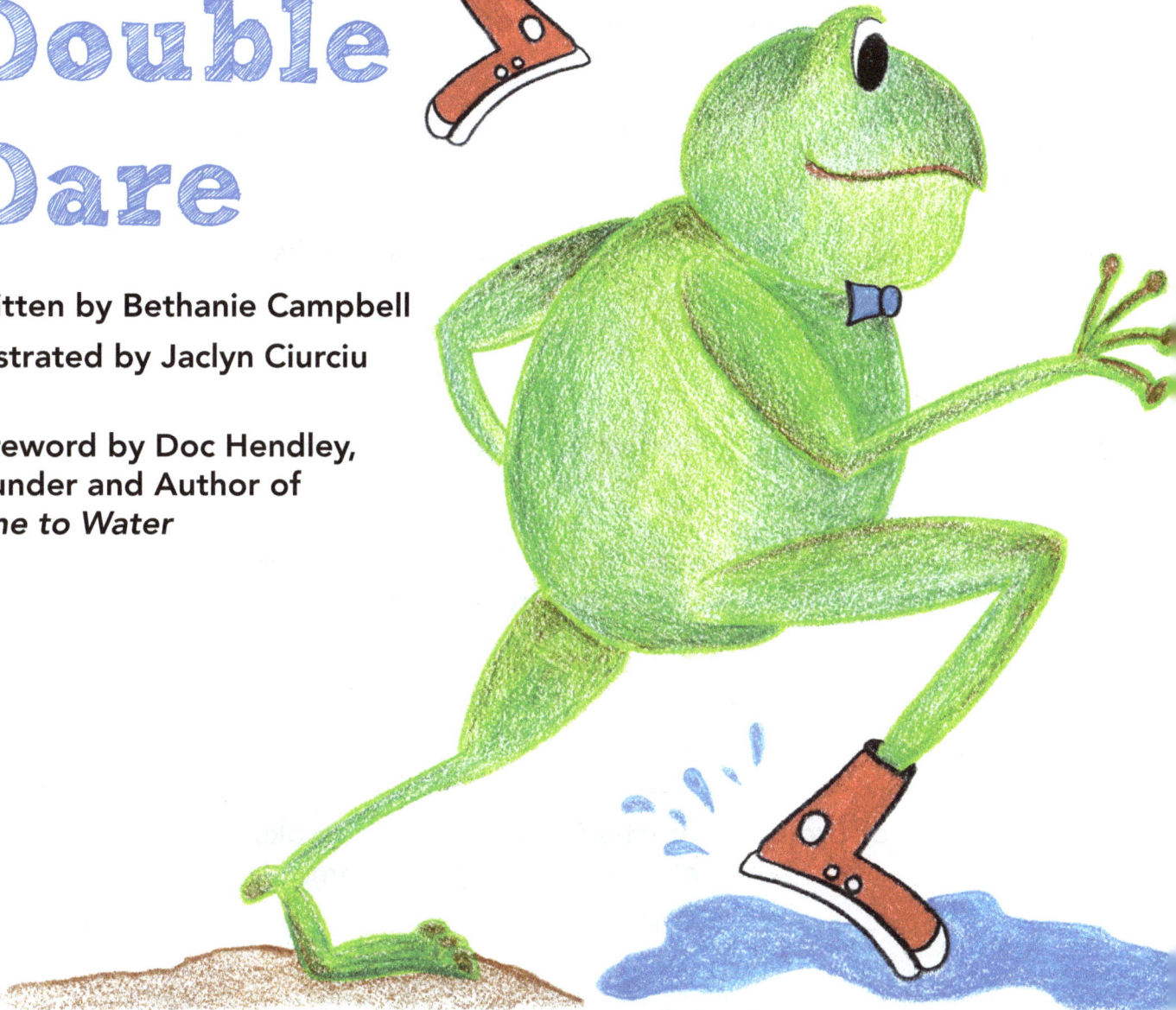

ISBN: 978-1-935256-21-2

Published by BackDoor Books
PO Box 1652
Boone, NC 28607

Illustrated by Jaclyn Ciurciu

Graphic design by Abbie Frease
abbiefrease.com

For ordering directly from BackDoor Books contact us
at ledgepress@gmail.com.

Dedication

First and foremost we would like to dedicate this book to Wine to Water and to everyone who has and who continues to devote their time and resources to water projects. Your efforts make it possible to help others with one of life's most basic needs—water. A portion of our book sales will go directly to Wine to Water so they can continue their projects in countries throughout the world.

I dedicate this book to my son, Roman Joseph and my little angel on the way.

— J.C.

I dedicate this book to God and my little Grum, Grum; Olivia Grace. You are both my inspiration and I love you so very much. To my family and friends, thank you for your love and support.

— B.C.

Foreword

"The water and sanitation crisis claims more lives through disease than any war claims through guns. More children die from water related illnesses than AIDS, malaria, and measles combined. Every 20 seconds a child dies from a water-related disease (2006 United Nations Human Development Report)."

These are just a few of the sobering facts that moved me to action back in 2003 and lead to the creation of Wine To Water. It has been an exciting, yet difficult and even dangerous journey at times fighting this world's water crisis but there is no doubt in my mind that every step along the way has been worth it.

One of the things that have shocked me the most through all of this is how much of an impact one everyday individual can have on this world. It doesn't matter who you are, where you are from, or what you've accomplished in life, everyone has the ability to have an extraordinary impact on the world around them.

That is exactly why I am so happy about this book. Not only is it helping to get the word out about the worlds water crisis to this next generation in a fun and exciting way, it is also helping to teach our children that anyone, even little Freddy Sinclair can make a difference.

Bethanie has done an amazing job of creating an adventure and a character that the reader can't help but fall in love with. I can't wait to see the impact this book will have not only on the lives of those who read it but also on my work at Wine To Water. I'm certain that once you've read it, you too will want to join us in fighting this world's water crisis.

For that, I am forever grateful for Ms. Bethanie Campbell.

Doc Hendley
Author of *Wine to Water*

INTRODUCING MR. FREDD

Hi, my name is Freddy, Freddy Sinclair.

I have a story that I'm eager to share.

It's about a journey that was amazing and fun.

So, sit down, sit tight, I have only begun!

You see, boys and girls, it
all started out—

One day in the forest
while
I was leaping about.

When suddenly I landed
straight down on a fist—

That was tightened around
a written up list.

The author was Barkley,
Barkley the Bear,

Who offered me cash on
a double dare.

So, I opened the list, the
list from his fist.

"The rules are as follows,"
he did insist.

RULES FOR THE DOUBLE DARE

Travel through
two countries
in 20 days.

What you can
take...NOTHING!!

Reward= $100 bucks

Mr. Barkley, one question, is there something you missed?

There are things that I need that are not on this list.

Surely I can take some food and some water?

I'm certain a backpack would **NOT** be a bother?

"Mr. Sinclair I inform you there is **NOTHING** that I missed.

I **KNOW** what I put on the list from my fist.

You must travel through two countries in twenty days flat,

With nothing at all and **NO** backpack on your back!

Food and water are things you must find,

Surely you'll be fine because people are kind."

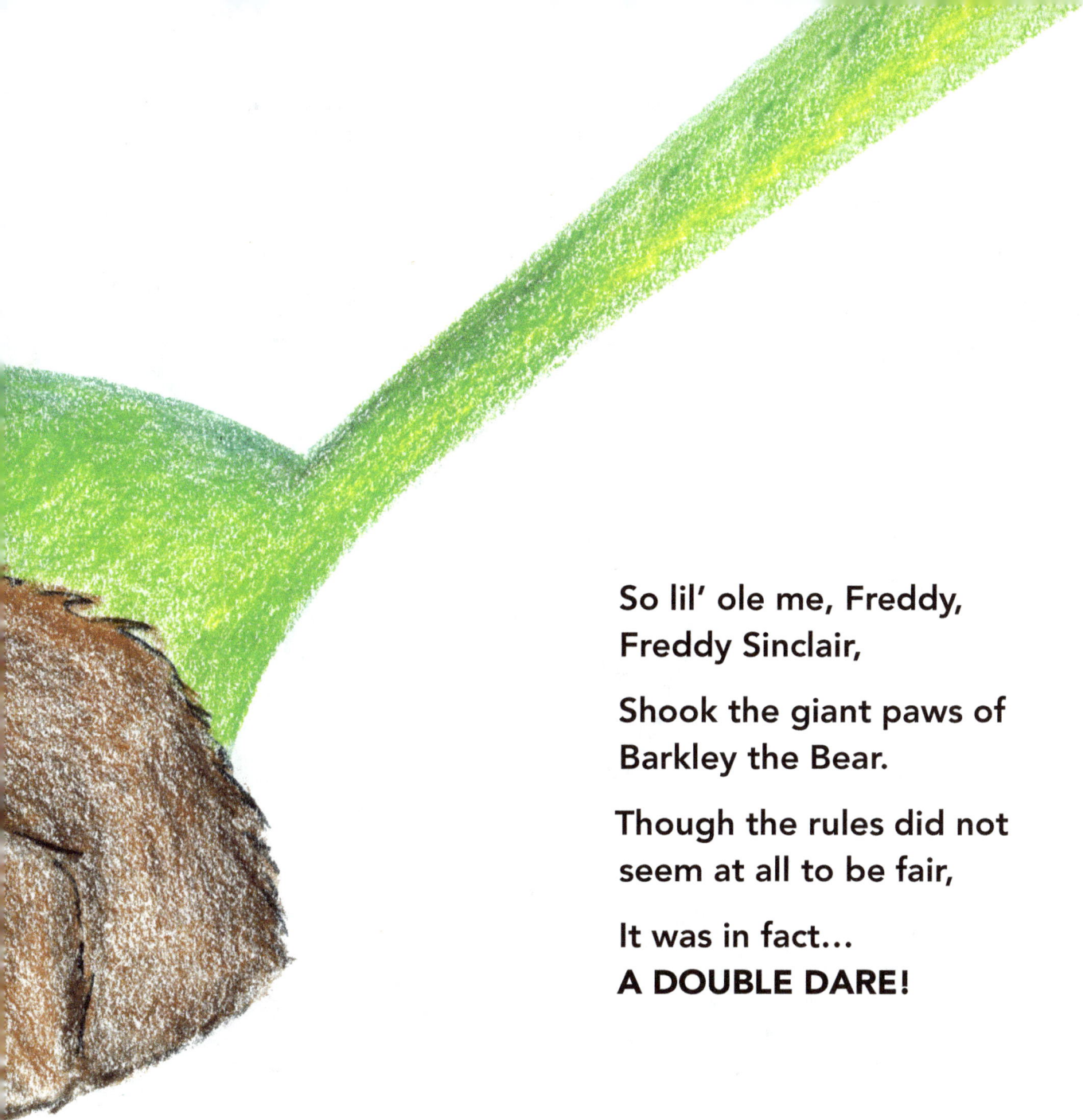

So lil' ole me, Freddy,
Freddy Sinclair,

Shook the giant paws of
Barkley the Bear.

Though the rules did not
seem at all to be fair,

It was in fact...
A DOUBLE DARE!

I started my journey
through the U. S. of A,

While ribbetting the tune
of Yip, Yip, Hooray!

I traveled by ship and got
tossed in some waves,

I surfed and I snorkeled
all during my days.

SHOES

When my belly would
rumble there were
plenty of flies,

And water was
everywhere for me
to survive.

Some nights I would hop to a nearby house.

I silenced my ribbett. I was quiet as a mouse.

I waited for mommas to tuck children to sleep,

Then I slurped from their water without making a peep.

So far I loved this wonderful land.

I felt like a prince. I felt very grand!

When days were stressful I drew a hot bath,

Or hopped into machines when I needed a laugh.

I loved to swim and sunbathe by the pool.

The kids thought that I was **SUPER** cool.

A day without soccer with my new friends was rare.

So far I did like Mr. Barkley's old dare.

The first ten days flew by like a breeze.

I was certain the next ten

would go by

with great ease.

Just then Sally Sparrow flew by in midair.

I asked for a ride and she didn't seem to care.

So, we flew and we flew through mornings of dew;

A bump was my cue that we'd landed some place new.

I tried looking around the land that awaits,

But it was hard to see, for the hour was late.

There was no brightness of light, only stars in the sky,

I stretched out my limbs waiting for night to fly by.

When daylight appeared
I arose with a stare,

To tents scattered around;
the land was so bare.

I leaped all around; I searched
through and through—

Until I found a fella that
I could talk to.

"Hi! My name is Freddy,
Freddy Sinclair.

Is there a bottle of water or
some food you can spare?"

He just kept on walking,
with his head held down.

There was no smile on his face,
just a very large frown.

"What happened," I thought, "To the wonderful land—

Where things came easy, where everything was grand?

Now I am walking on sun scorched sand,

In a village named Marla, in western Sudan."

There was no machine to get a cheap thrill.

No left out water, not even a spill.

There were no kids at school, no sign of a pool,

No soccer, no friends, I was no longer cool.

At night I could munch on bugs that I had found,

But water was nowhere, not even a sound.

I followed some ladies in bright yellow clothing.

I was curious to find out where they were going.

They carried large tubs on top of their heads.

Their faces determined, no word was said.

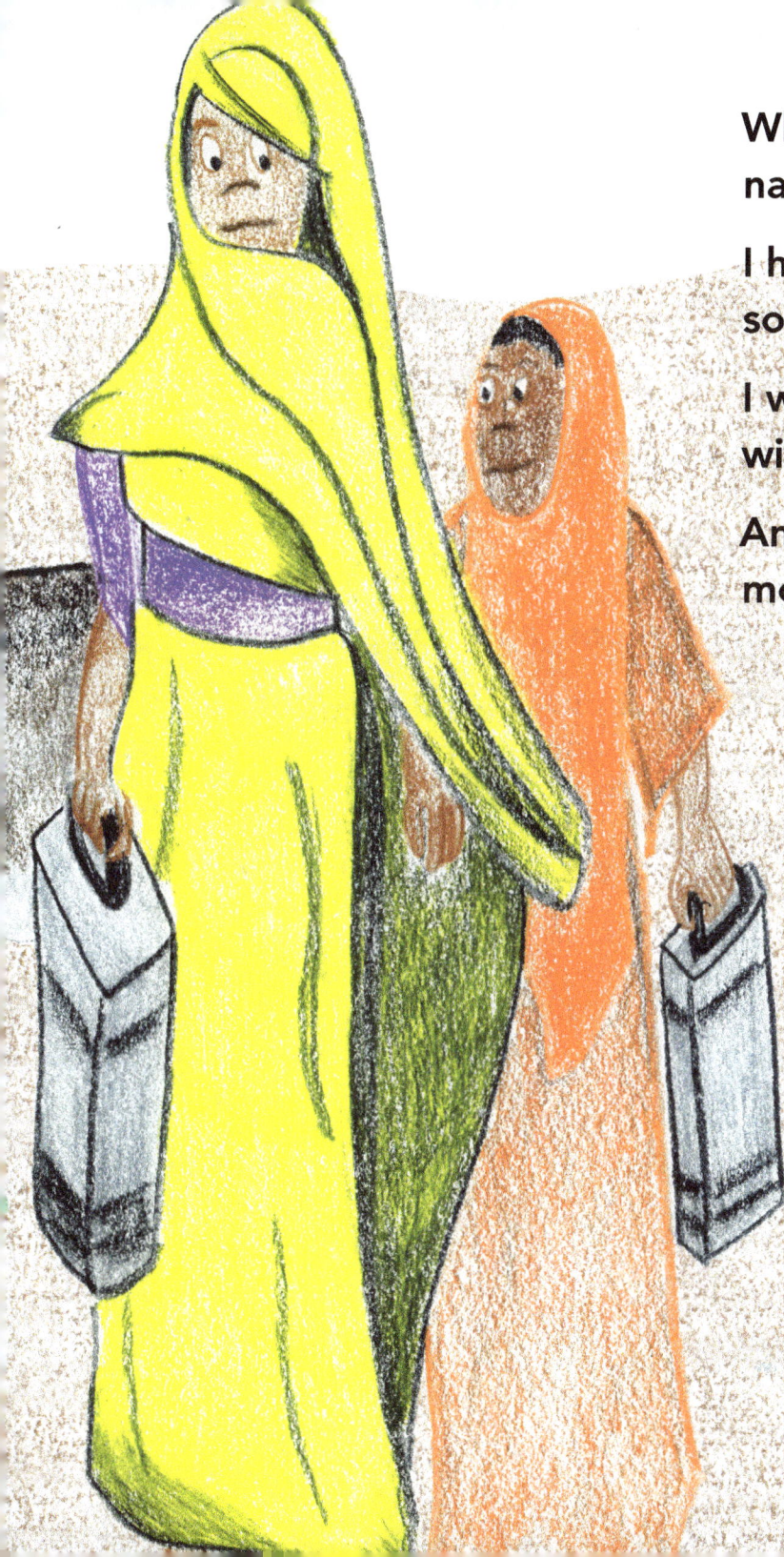

When we finally arrived at a small, narrow creek—

I had to jump in, for I was feeling so weak.

I watched as each tub filled up with brown water,

And placed on the heads of both mothers and daughters.

We walked back for miles, hours upon hours.

My body was aching, I no longer had power.

That night I was **SOO** sick. I developed the sweats.

I was hot with a fever, my skin dripping wet.

My head was pounding. I could no longer thrive.

Three more days; how could I survive?

I closed my eyes and counted sheep.

All I wanted was to fall fast asleep.

The next morning I was wakened by an unusual tune.

Clapping and laughter and smiles were in bloom.

A circle crowded around a convoy of men;

They kept coming and coming in groups of ten.

Eyes were set on one man alone,

Who was drilling the earth, into its bone.

His arms began pumping, first up and then down.

His movement then brought the most beautiful sound.

A splash of water trickled down through his hand.

It watered the cracks, it softened the land.

The people of Marla arose in loud cheer.

Eyes were flowing with jubilant tears.

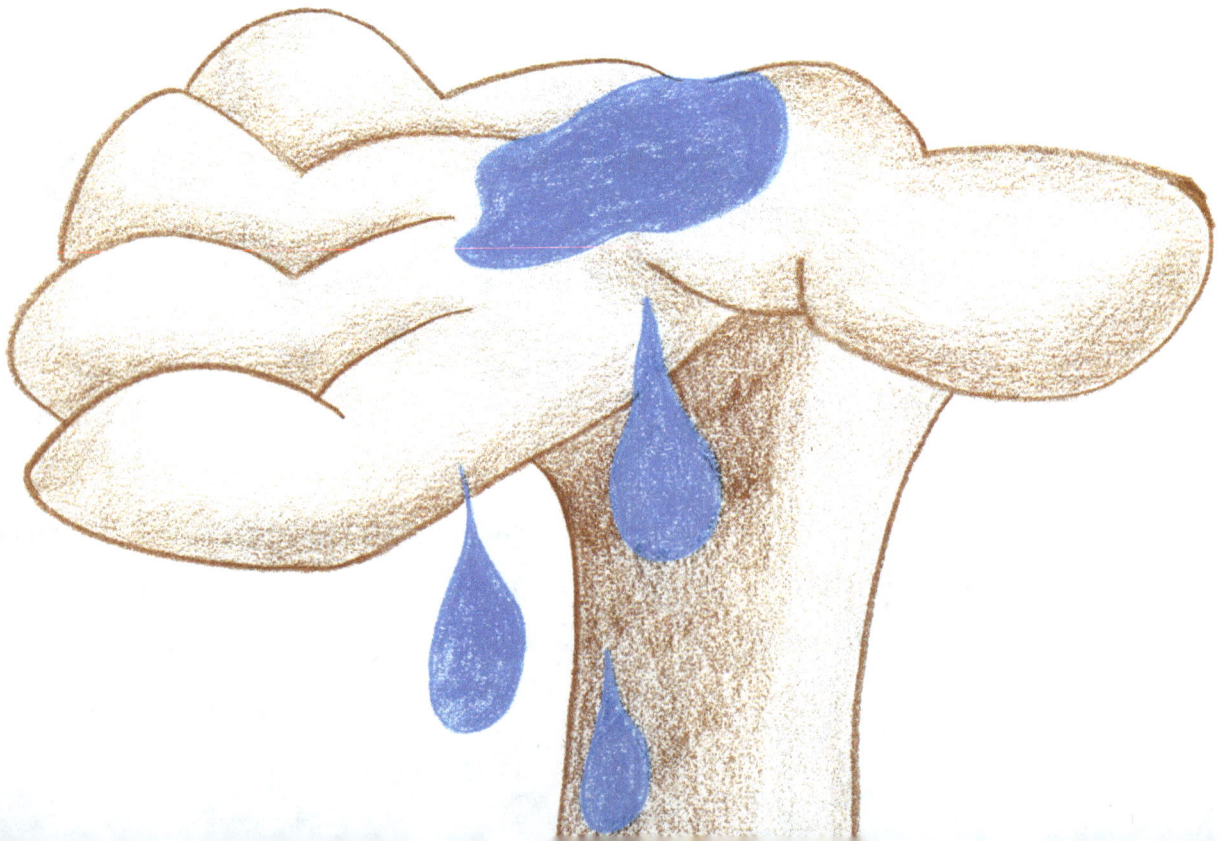

The next two days I will never forget,

The village was stirring with the gift that was sent.

I realized that day I was no longer the same.

This journey had become much more than a game.

My heart had grown, my purpose was new;

I wanted to tell others who hadn't a clue.

So, I leaped in the suitcase of the mysterious man,

Who brought clean water to Sudan's dry land.

I slid deep down, into his dirty old boot.

The smell made my ribbit go from loud to mute.

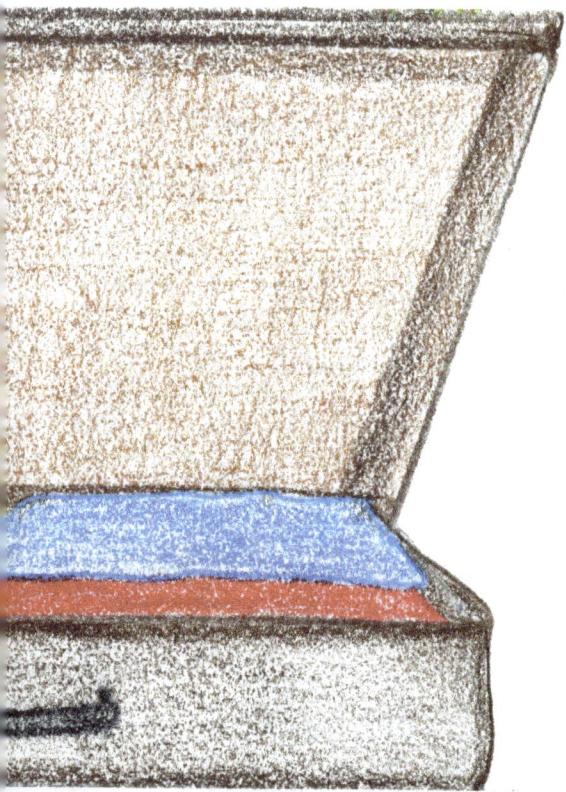

We arrived hours later to a house full of laughter,

That echoed through the walls and the wooden rafters.

I watched the man scoop up his little boys,

Who were beaming with smiles, beaming with joy.

He kissed his lady on top of her head,

"I love you, I love you," is all that she said.

I snuck out their window and hurried back home,

I was eager to share the world I had known.

For hours I ribbited and for hours I rambled,

To birds and reptiles and a circle of mammals.

At the end of my story Barkley stood with a stare.

He seemed to be smiling, he seemed to care.

"Here is 100 bucks to a frog from a bear.

Nice job finishing your double dare."

My journey taught me lessons like to help and to share,

So I filled out a check and signed, "Freddy Sinclair."

I wanted my earnings to help in some way,

And brighten another village again someday.

The End

The Author

Writing came early for Bethanie. At six she discovered her passion for writing when the sounds and prosody of language fascinated her. During her teenage years she often found herself lost in a poem by Emily Dickenson or Robert Frost and often running wild with a story by Dr. Suess. Then, at the young age of 20 came the birth of her daughter, Olivia Grace who further opened her eyes to a world of wonder and words. Crazy ideas, elaborate adventures and splendid characters came rushing to her mind after giving her daughter a bath or playing with her. It was within these moments that she hurried to capture these images on paper.

This excitement with words, ideas and a swelling desire to share her imaginations lead her to finish her Bachelor's degree in Elementary Education. Later she followed with a Master's degree in Reading Education. Her future dreams are for more education and lots of writing.

She writes in moments between being a mom, working at Appalachian State University, tutoring and numerous odd jobs. A great sense of accomplishment comes when she is able to create a story that leaves a lasting impression on readers. For her, this accomplishment came when the story of "Freddy Sinclair's Double Dare" was completed.

To order copies contact BackDoor Books

PO Box 1652
Boone, NC 28607

828.406.0469
ledgepress@gmail.com

www.ingramcontent.com/pod-product-compliance
Lightning Source LLC
Chambersburg PA
CBHW081258110426

42743CB00045B/3334